NIXES MATE REVIEW

ISSUE 28/29 SUMMER/FALL 2023

Nixes Mate Publications
Allston, Masssachusetts

Book design by Michael McInnis.
Cover image used with permission.

Philip Borenstein ·Publisher Emeritus

Hannah Larrabee · Editor + Explorer

Michael McInnis · Designer + Factotum

Annie Elezabeth Pluto · Editor + Director

ISBN 978-1-949279-48-1

Nixes Mate Publications
POBox 1179
Allston, MA 02134
nixesmate.pub

We're tight into hurricane season here at Nixes Mate Headquarters. No better time than to sit with our Summer/Fall 2023 issue and read your way through family dilemmas, ekphrastics, and the spirits of color and place. We have 18 writers newly joining the Nixes Mate family. In the future, we hope to read more of their work. We are happy to announce that Hannah Larrabee, who guest edited our climate change issue back in 2021, has joined our editorial staff. In addition to editorial duties, Hannah is our *Explorer*.

Table of Contents

How to not be scared · Natalie Jill

Think of all the creatures evolution never created. The universe took this long to make you; it can't unmake you now.

Notice parsley on the counter, yellowing like autumn.

Catch the moment streetlights flick on, beginning their midnight guard.

Watch how inky sunsets get from forest fire particulate. Interference makes beauty.

Glance up at the moon: there are footsteps there too. Gaze at the milky way, stemming your arms like flowers towards all that light.

Your heart doesn't need your help to beat.

Whatever happens, make it a poem.

I gave My breath to the Dodo. It was never yours
alone. I loved those birds: quiet, curious, unafraid.
What did you make of their example? Slaughter,
for meat you called insipid, laughing at their wings.

Xerces Blue: My lilac, chestnut, cobalt
butterflies, among the dunes. Their larvae fed
on lupins, sand-spread lotus, in their only home.
You claim to miss them. Your bulldozers don't.

You ask Me to dispense salvation
as if I were a robot fortune teller.
But you refuse to overthrow your lives.
You pray to Me with tongues of shrapnel.

And there's a question: in which of those six days
did I call shrapnel good? Approve the landmine?
It's been an age since I perused that book.
Tell Me. Whose heaven will you frack

with buried, flightless arms? The mountaintops
will weep for joy when all of you are gone.

Elegy for Snaefellsjökull Glacier · Sara Letourneau

Snaefellsnes Peninsula, Iceland, September 2021

You will likely die before I die.
I was not thinking of this when I was standing in
the black-gravel pull-off along Route 574,
pressing the smartphone camera's button every few seconds
in case the previous photo was blurry.
In that moment, you were making an appearance,
cooperating with the cloudless late-summer sky
and shifting your volcano's lenticular scarf to the right
so I could see you. White as an Arctic fox in winter,
your body of ice was dense and seemingly stationary.
Later, upon checking my photos, I discovered that
your beautiful crevasses and river-waves –
the details I'd seen with the naked eye
and hoped to capture by zooming in –
were almost invisible. Instead,
the black necks of lava rock protruding from your summit
bade me not to look away.
Those rocks are ill omens, I've since been told.
They were first sighted nine years ago
because you are melting.

There is no end I can conceive for myself
that can equal the agony of yours:

dissolving from the fluid, frozen state
you reveled in for 700,000 years,
down to the sickly four square miles that's left,
growing thinner and thinner until
you're too frail to flow,
while watching your sisters in Iceland and beyond
disintegrate in the same way.
All the while, you're sitting with the creeping knowledge
that the world will one day be an enormous jökulhlaup –
those glacial dam bursts you know so well –
swallowing shorelines,
flooding coastal houses and businesses,
displacing and drowning their residents,
and depriving us of the many gifts
you and your siblings share with us,
like irrigation and fertile soil for our crops,
freshwater for our thirst,
and cold air to balance our climate.

I wish I could hold you out of comfort,
tell you that the future might not be so bad.
But what would make your passing worse:
The lie to ease your pain?
Or the tender, well-intended gesture?
The warmth I create – not with my heart,
but with my hands, my car, my electricity –
is only bringing your eviction date closer.
I am thirty-seven years old,

and if the estimates hold true,
you will likely die before I die, and now I know
that the rivulets and waterfalls I spotted
while driving along your peninsula's coast
are not meltwater,
but the tear-streams of a grandmother,
crying her last.

At six thirty her children rolled their eyes.
You already told us that story.
Martha was tired, lingering and selfish,
she walked off to the park.

She closed her eyes and saw a pattern of crosses
and beneath the geometry was a gorgeous magenta,
slightly darkened by the evening sky.
Somewhere near the end of summer and early fall, she threw the flowers from their pots
near the pine and erected a geranium gravesite
where populations were thrown without ceremony in dark earth.

I'm enjoying a night on the town. No thanks to those squiggly eels, I've got my own slippery style. Of course, everybody is famous now, although you can barely tell one from the other, so it's pretty much unanimous. Suffering loves company, especially if you're sick and tired of the same old same old. But look who's talking.

Tuesday, my cousin Billy, that snake, swallowed himself. As a brand ambassador, it was the least he could do. Fortunately, there'll be no more counting backward in alphabetical order for Lonesome Billy. In fact, he quit the whole vegan thing and prefers plastic flowers to hydroponic gardening, at least until he gets back on his feet.

It's impossible to know where you are without being somewhere in time. The First World War wasn't the First World War, until the Second World War. The future mutilates the past, which is why I can't tell if I'm taking the pre-test or the post-test? I guess it depends on my net worth.

Whenever I'm away from home, I like to practice my evasive driving skills. It doesn't matter who you run into; it only matters who runs into you. Of course, wherever you are, you must pay attention to the magnetic waves. Remember: at the South Pole, every direction is north. No matter how hard they try, they'll never take that away from you.

Toni Artuso · **A Cross Dresser Marries**

She   caressed him. Thrilled by a female touch, he
thought,   *She loves me.* But he was desperate.
If I just   *pledge my heart*, he hoped she'd not
touch his clothes.   She could cure his desire to dress.
I will be healed   *then*, he convinced himself.

At once   she sensed something amiss, saw her chance.
Jesus,   she thought, *I'll hoard this weapon.* She
realized that power   lay with her. Secret
had gone out from him,   beyond his recall.

He turned   out to be true, building his life
around   their kids, suppressing his urges
in the crowd   of responsibilities

and   it worked – for a while. Then one day, he
asked, "Who   cuckolds me?" She countered, "Why've you
touched my clothes?"   as if that settled the score.

– Mark 5:28b & 30,
New International Version

The Moon is My NonBinary Mirror · Meghan Sterling

A small unfurling, like hair from a woman's
legs. A man's legs. The thick of the calves,

the rope of the thighs. My woman-man legs
wrapped around spring, its tendrils coming

through the forest floor with a whisper like
the moon. The moon was always my lover

in the spring. Was never. I thought she was so *she*.
I wanted her to be a him. I wanted the him of her,

coarseness shaved away, leaving that shadow with
its delicate pocks. The tender her in him, that wide white bone.

Two of us inside the one. A forest of moons, where beneath
the canopy, there is light. See how things grow: a fern

like a baby reaching out of the vast nest of its mother.
The thin fern cresting, its body made alive with hair like

nerves. A woman who survived cancer once told a friend,
"I will never shave my body again," like she was new,

curls in every corner, vibrant, thick with health. Why
would I want to be rid of it? My birthright, my sex.

Why should the moon **have** to choose? The forest knows.
The bud comes to us in a coating of fur.

Susan Tepper · **With Rain**

Often it begins with rain
when contemplating backward

a morning consumed not by love
or random touching beneath covers

the drain pipe slurping
what is too much to contain
without sagging in the middle

Slipping downstairs
I cough into my sleeve –
not to awaken the house

entering his 9 by 9 space
still crushed / not yet reconfigured

Because They Remind Me of My Mother's Dementia
I Throw Away the Pussy Willows · Cindy Veach

For two years they sat with me at the Formica table,
ate with me, read with me, wrote with me. But today,
when I look at them I see cobwebs connecting
one catkin to the next and then they turn into furry
Cossack hats and the photo of my mother wearing one
when they were the rage in the sixties. Where was she standing?
Which house? Which two children at her side?
She can't remember. I'm ashamed; afraid this will happen
to me. I touch one of the catkins and it falls off. I touch
another and it falls off. These stems denied water, not allowed
to bloom, have lived in a time warp, in a perpetual early spring –
a trove of vintage hats, an eternally budding army standing
at attention – my lost mother, forever stylish and beautiful
in her beloved Cossack cap.

Trowels in stiff-gloved hands, my neighbors
bend over raised beds, transplant
geraniums, circle their azaleas
with blood meal and chicken manure.

I bend over the page or laptop, open
another book, try out lines, hoping a poem
will take root. If I transplant too early
the fragile germ will fizzle out.

Too much enthusiasm will wither it.
I want it, like my elderly rhododendron,
to un-origami fever-bright blooms from
tight buds, can't bear to sit in the same room.

Doom is woven into beginnings: pots
crumble, Spanish bluebells take over
the yard. I fear the eagerness of my voice.
Scrape back to bare soil, trowel rusted,

pen leaking ink. April teases senses
dulled by winter's dusty darkened spaces
with its fragrant extravagance, naked
call – is it, am I – cruel after all?

The Terrible Passions · Rebecca Connors

"I have tried to express the terrible passions of humanity by means of red and green."
– *Vincent Van Gogh in a letter about* The Night Cafe

Lust is a razor, a red-eye flight, berries bursting on the vine.
Give-take.

You love me. A stoked oven pulses low in my body –
I hunt you.   No, I offer myself up – a feast in this verdant glen.

Moss, fern, forest, emerald, spring – I am a dominant wavelength.

The Valentines I send you are red. Watching you receive others
makes me green.

You love me not.   What lure could I use?
My heart   that devil has red horns, wears a green coat–
                            has to be a likable fellow–

how else will you take the bait? How else will you move those lips
towards me,
                            suckle this push-pull between us?

A blood meal stirred in soil nurtures your trees like
the ardency of your hips   flushes my sallow skin.

You love me like a rose petal ripped screaming from its crown.

My vermillion lips part.		All these days I have waited –
Another tug			as this green wind knocks me

to the ground: *You love me not*. You splendid and triumphant,
come to claim another.
			Celadon scales spark shimmer as I breathe dragon-fire,
			blistering your honey-tongue.

Lust is battle-scarred,
			burnt crust, mottled grapes.

Jaded. Exposed to the elements – my heart my rage my –

& yet,		unaware of all I have ravaged

spring tendrils emerge,
			daffodils & iris dotted among the charred trees.

Lavender Honey · R. A. Allen

I was in Paris
France.
On the plane over,
I decided to gather material
for a Paris guidebook.
Something anti-Gopnikian.
Something to confirm the rudeness
of Parisians who pretend not to speak
English when Americans ask
where to buy a jar of *miel de lavande*.
Diligently – but unsuccessfully –
I searched for rude Frenchpersons.
My guidebook was deliquescing
into a pamphlet. Eventually,
I realized my frog-gigging gambits
were flawed. Opening with "Bonjour"
(while flashing a list of Francophrases)
actually averts Yank-aversion
A modicum of respect
is like nectar for bees.

On my final day, I was royally insulted
by the maître d' at Les Deux Musées.
He was *un connard* that any American
could hate & appreciate. I had to love
him. Not worth a guidebook, but
at least I came home with this poem.

Jennifer Martelli

a review of *People Once Real by* Richard Hoffman

Lily Poetry Review Press, 2023

In his poem, "Mundus et Infans," Richard Hoffman writes,

> People once real, who'd loved their lives, and one another,
> who might not have meant to harm but only warn me –
> in what first tongue did I compose those poems. . . .

Hoffman confronts his own "child in the world," invoking – and evoking – a poetic lineage. His latest collection, *People Once Real*, secures Hoffman's place in this cosmology; his voice is brave and inquisitive, searching for the right words to plumb the depths of his own American existence. The collection engages with politics, with childhood before language, and finally, as the child in the world. Hoffman masterfully shifts the landscape from poet of witness to child confronting the adults who witnessed atrocities, and yet remained silent. This is a book of language from the epistolary poem addressed to Walt Whitman to the final words spoken by a child, the granddaughter, watching ants, *That his dead/brother he/ bringing him home.*

In the first section, "Mundus," Hoffman describes the inadequacies of poetic witness. In "The Hole," he writes

"There's a hole in this poem. . . .

a hole that allows the loud world
to decide which portion of itself
to poke through and require me
to describe it or address it. . . .

The "hole" becomes a portal, allowing the speaker to travel across political landscapes, as well as temporal. Only a poet with Hoffman's mastery of language can guide the reader this securely through the constant gaslighting. Writing a villanelle with the ease of Elizabeth Bishop, Hoffman uses this obsessive form to wrangle selfishness, self-preservation, and witness. In "How to Get By," a poem prompted by the murder of "135 Black unarmed people nationwide" at the hands of police officers, he tells us

> Forget what you've seen, and for your own sake,
> give up understanding what you've understood.
> Call it an accident, not hatred. Call it a mistake.

Adhering to the rules of the form, the repeated lines travel through the poem, echoing the concept of the unreliability of words (sake, mistake, fake, opaque, heartache), until they land at that chilling end, "to think your outrage, anger, your heartache,/if spoken, might change anything or do any good." As a poet, the idea that words are unreliable, or worse, unattainable, is nightmarish. Hoffman's "dreamed of world" balances on the edge of these opposing concepts – needing words, yet not able to access them. In "Tenebrae," which references the three days before Easter, the speaker, "a wisp of smoke from cold ashes" attempts to describe this un-language,

> Everything my father feared, all that my mother
> knew but could not say *Pulvis et umbra summus,*
>
> use and meaning the same, no use to know good,
> some tide pulling love away, exposing words
>
> meant to hold together several generations to see
> further. . . .

Part II, "Infans," refers, not only to childhood, but to the period of childhood before language. In this section, the landscape appears to change: now we are in the speaker's boyhood. The trauma of political, racial, and economic violence in Part I reappear as the young boy sexually assaulted and as the boy whose brother has died. These remembered traumas remain "inside the outline of my shadow always/as per our agreement." The poet of societal witness becomes the poet of personal witness, trying to find words for childhood trauma, as well as questioning the responsibility of the adults. Hoffman shifts the perspective from the speaker observing the world to the adults observing the assault of a child. The poem "Formica" begins with sound, "I'm eleven. My father hears me say "fuck,"/and decides it's time for the talk." Hoffman underscores the inadequacy of words,

> He said it was holy. He didn't know
> my coach with his crooked *organ* had already
> *inflamed* my pretty body, burned me to ash.

Hoffman's longer poem in this section, "A Prayer for the Souls of Purgatory," is a slow turning to – if not love – than forgiveness. The poems asks, "If he had cried out, that boy,/would anyone have heard?" Writing the poem as prayer and interrogation, Hoffman ends with

> I forgive
>
> their inattention: not one of them
> from whom I would
> withhold untroubled dying.

These poems of memory are the most heartbreaking in their attempts to reconcile the speaker's own trauma with those who traumatized. In "Bobber," the speaker, observing two boys fishing, feels the shame of loneliness and poverty, and of missing his brother. This causes him to want to "hurt one of them badly."

This brotherless boy emerges in the last section, "Mundus et Infans," a 12-part poem that takes on the carelessness of adults, acting as frivolously as children. As "the child in the world," the speaker revisits the political and familial traumas, this time, confronting a refusal to witness. In section 5, "Mundus et Infans," the speaker challenges

> Ideas, not children,
> that have never matured, impossible,
> equating helplessness with innocence,
> wordless amnesia with paradise. . .

In this final section, Hoffman's invocations include border guards separating children, King Herod who ordered the slaughter of babies, and Isaac, who was almost sacrificed by his father.

The second part of the poem, "Art a Great Investment, Says Forbes," weaves the portrait "The Massacre of the Innocents" with images of children being sacrificed, "A recurrent theme in western art." Hoffman quotes the words of the border guards, who say, "it is hard/to separate mothers." The child in the world – or the child in war – is wise, yet ineffective. Iphigenia, the daughter who was sacrificed at the start of the Trojan War is invoked by Hoffman: she "makes prophecy," and in the end, "knows the harm they will do/and that no words will stop them."

People Once Real is a collection that digs down to the tongue-root of pre-language and language – with all its mercurial qualities. Time is circular in this book: children harmed by gunfire, poverty, geo-politics, become the child abused by adults in schools and in the church, traumatized by the death of a sibling. In "Raptor," Hoffman tells us, *To be truthful is to remember and grieve.* The poetic sense in this book brings the reader to a place of truth, but also deeper understanding of ourselves. Richard Hoffman has led us across a landscape many of us know, and has made the journey a bit kinder, a bit lovelier.

Miriam O'Neal

Baffling Light: a review of *In the Book I'm Reading* by Mary Kane

One Bird Books (2023)

In The Book I'm Reading: Stories, is a small, jewel-like collection of stories by poet and fiction writer, Mary Kane. Kane's work is reminiscent of Mary Ruefle's for its droll humor and poignant intelligence, but her voice is distinct from Ruefle's, marked as it is with interior landscapes that feel both large and intimate. You can see the pairings in these opening sentences. They can't help but occur because these stories occur as two hands clapping, a left and a right, a pasta pot and its strainer, Proust and Kafka. We leap from known to unknown, from the human anatomy of tibia, femur, molar, clavicle, to an imagined interior world where doors and windows open or shut within the human frame. The stories in *In The Book...* range from a single sentence to 4-6 pages tops. "Well Into It" is a single sentence:

Well into our marriage I learn that before we met, you were a champion bowler.

Perhaps it doesn't sound like a 'jewel' as mentioned in the first sentence of this review. However, set, as it is, between an ornate little story about "reading in bed and snow [ ] falling outside" in which the speaker/reader imagines Camus "sitting in his study, looking out the window" and "A New Old Couple" in which a husband and wife just lying down to sleep notice all at once, how each looks like her/his father and lie "side by side, two old men holding hands in the dark", "Well Into It" is lit with a kind of baffling, quotidian light.

Certain characters reappear at intervals not to be relied upon. For example, there is Mr. Leopold. In one story, he is in Tucson, visiting a friend. In another story, he is in his basement, which is where, "it is estimated, he spends 39% of his time," painting as he "orbits several large pieces of paper laid on the floor...". There is the husband who is afraid of poetry and must be rescued from it by his wife, who plucks it, barehanded, from the counter and reads it.

Reading is both subject and activity in these stories. 'The Joys of Reading' ruminates over the speaker's admission that it's difficult to read 'for information.' In fact, most facts hardly stick at all. We find out that

> While I might expect not to be able to remember what year Martin Luther pinned his 95 Theses to the church door, or the distance from the earth to the moon, my condition, if that's what one calls it, persists even when the information in question delights me, such as what year Gertrude Stein moved to 27 Rue de Fleurus in Paris and when she stopped wearing those awful puffy Gibson Girl blouses and skirts that really didn't suit her...And what year Marcel Proust hired two boxes at the theater and threw a party for his friends, celebrating his retreat from social life to begin writing *In Search of Lost Time* in a fur coat in his bed under seven woolen blankets (64).

In The Book I'm Reading is small enough to slip into a large pocket or a small purse. But its physical size belies the size of this collection and the worlds a reader may enter and exist within story by story. Lovers of literature will love these stories where Flannery O'Connor and the Hang Dynasty get cameo appearances. But also, lovers of musing, readers of multiple disciplines at once, those interested in the history of dentistry or who have ever wondered about the relationship between Roy Rogers and his Palomino, Trigger will also find something to chew on. In short, any reader who delights in the way words can make a stew of the quotidian and the fantastic will be charmed and heartened by these small countries of the subconscious and the imagination.

"Mujer Angel, Desierto de Sonora" · Deb Leipziger

I cannot see your face –
all I see are your arms curved in blessing.
You are blessing the desert.

Your hair rivers down your back,
the land dry as parchment and leather,
full of marvels.

Heat cuts the day,
your clothes cinched at the waist.
You rise up, like mountains.

Your head cast down, reverent,
a gathering of strength
which you give to me.

In your right hand, perhaps
a suitcase, small with
belonging.

The desert sings your song.

This poem is based on a photograph from the National Museum of Women in the Arts by Graciela
Iturbide entitled "Mujer Ángel, Desierto de Sonora" (Angel Woman, Sonoran Desert)

scratch the brine of a scabbed itch;
the sun bakes perfectly square
patches of my neighbor's lawn,
and the smell of hay
becomes my madeleine.

At the Arboretum, Linda and I sneak
through meadows of asters and
rye grass, hide from gardeners
on the steep slope of white pine
near the Forest Hills Gate.

The grass blades slice our fingers,
leave blood on fuzzy seed heads
as we snatch handfuls to push through
the chain link fence to horses indentured
to the Massachusetts Biological Laboratory.

Horses languid and deliberate in their patience;
long eyelashes studded with August flies
like moving glitter on a Mardi Gras mask.
They nibble our meager oblations
with velvet lips; they are so beautiful in this.

They are Black Beauty and Flicka
escaped from the page. We are
girls lost in families indifferent to story's
rhyme, and even then I knew
we could never be cowboys.

Philip Montenegro · **Hotel Room**

after Edward Hopper

Time and again I recall
burying whispers in your hair,
two silhouettes
telling lies to each other
in the candor of our sheets.

Although there are bright countries calling opportunity to single pairs of legs, like magazines
       yelling "I can make you desirable, wealthy, and satisfied in the sack,"
Although I will wear away like gregarious patinas from Greek sculpture, standing cross and plain
       as a salt block,
Although dirt mounds sleep like weasels against our apartment windows,
Although no flowers will tilt dog-like heads from the table, panting spontaneity,
Although threads are yanked from the patchwork quicker than we can stitch, although gaps have
       been and will be snipped where we most need warmth and pattern,
Although smaller, smarter, blonder lovers will haunt your biological needs,
Although there are disks overhead transporting ominous messages only certain professionals can
       translate - although we are not among them,
Although ages of reproduction teach impermanence as the only rule of tenderness,
Although tenderness is in the eye of the beholder,
Although the holder of our little lives cares no more for us than for the empty chrysalis clinging
       against the wind,
Although no one holds us at all,
Although the wind has been known to tell lies, leading men and women to unfamiliar
       landmarks - much like kites chauffeured to boughs, feathers sent swimming, poems
       released without edits to sidewalk,
Although expiration insists like clammy fingers into the apricot jam,
Although poems pull pieces of our life from me, morph them to warped exhibits of
       exclamation,
Although the stars are professors with plans for our betterment, no matter what sorrow their
       maps suggest,
I tether my boat to yours and offer our oars to the water.

Tim Suermondt · **Shallow Harbor**

The boat brings my wife and I
to the shore.
We grab our one suitcase
and walk over a series of wooden
planks that keep us
from stepping in mud and on
the tiny, strange creatures that inhabit it.
We don't know where we're going.
My wife points at a fleet of crows
flying fast.
"Let's go in their direction," she says,
and we do. Even though I'm aware
it's dangerous
to look back, I take a glance.
The city whose skyline I should be able
to see is not there, gone completely.
I'll miss
the streetlights most of all,
the sad yet romantic illumination
I bathed myself in for decades.
My wife and I follow a dirt road,
leading to
the future we can't trust but cherish.
The crows circle nearby
when we kiss.

My Honda broke down on the I-80
smoke a hundred cigarettes waiting
for the bus to take me out of Wyoming.
Being white, no policeman bothered me.

Hitchhiked through Utah headed for Denver,
a dozen desert hours spent with that trucker.
We spoke of Standing Rock and the bourgeoisie.
In this story, I got home safely.

See a man in bushes by a northern freeway
his way to shelter, healthcare, three meals a day.
In this wishful America no one gets deported,
and at-risk humans are all supported.

The pain of folks hurting is my fighting
for their rights and their dignity,
and the soul truth – my privilege lets me
choose which America is meant for me.

Hibiscus blossoms staining the ground,
the sound of chickens in the road,
one girl using a long root as a jump rope
and five piglets in a rock pile,

goats' bowed heads in the field,
truck tires submerged in red mud,
the glassy surface of a lake
on this windless day,

a wooden boat with three boys,
one with a carved paddle,
another pulling a long curl
of thick bark through water,

& in the hum of afternoon insects,
the goats cry out,
another language
I don't know.

My students, thirteen years old and small, black tudong tucked
around their faces, knocking on my bedroom windows, saying, Miss,
Miss, you must get up! The fog is coming! And I am mid-afternoon
nap, blurry with sleep. And the fog is coming, faster still
due to the jungle-rusted trucks the men are driving at a steady ooze
forward, into the heart of the neighborhood, the men in space suits carrying hoses
issuing forth blasts of blank white. Laura and I hide
the food, close the glass door, slip on our plastic shoes that slap the ground
with every step. We lock our gate and then run, the fog follows
disappearing our house, our car, our neighbors'
homes stand empty, are swallowed by opaque air.
And the fog keeps appearing
at every corner, a wall erasing our surroundings, herding us
further from our home, rendering the familiar neighborhood ghostly,
strange. The fog comes closer. It smells sharp,
cloying. We run past the field with the feral puppies we visit daily– their yips
are silent today– we sprint through the empty
playground. And then, at last, an alley.
Air finally transparent and shimmering in the warm light,
at its end: our favorite roadside stand, teh tarik and roti canai
while we wait. My students are already there, explain
the fog is to kill the bugs, the bugs that suck blood and carry diseases.
There has been disease here, and so something had to be done
about it, which is the fog.
It is simple, in this way.

The fog disperses finely into the air,
gaseous poison turning invisible in the sticky yellow
of late afternoon, bugs falling on linoleum, dead in its wake.

Good Pentecostals Don't Pierce Their Ears · Ammanda Moore

In the church, the body is God's temple; it shouldn't be marked or pierced or
decorated beyond its natural beauty.

But finally, at twenty-six years old, two little diamonds sparkled against my skin.

My mom entered the restaurant all smiles, her long hair wound up into a bun
like a little castle. It'd been months since I'd seen her.

A gasp.

"What've you done to your ears?" She shrieked, clutching her chest.

And then she was gone – locked away to grieve in the bathroom.

I touched my ear and grinned.

When she asked me if I was in love
with *that girl* – nineteen to my twenty-one –
when she coaxed the truth from me one Sunday
afternoon, my father in the basement watching football,
roast in the oven – when in that wounded voice
she said *your daddy and I are worried*

about you. And then when I said yes,
and what relief to speak the truth –
never having the freedom to lie, to hide
anything about myself from her prying eyes –
she said *I'm glad you feel good about this*
now that you've ruined our lives.

She said *it would be better if you were hooked*
on drugs. She said, *you're killing your father.*
She said, *whoever you told this, you tell them*
that it was a mistake, and you find some man to date.

She put her foot down. But this, she could not forbid
although she tried. When my brother said he didn't want
that – meaning me – around his children, she said
he was *devout*; I can't remember to what.

And that was the end of being her child for a very long while.

Later, when she needed me to care for her in her age,
she said: *I'm prouder of you than all my children.*

And what did she say to her other two?

I'd thought Grandmother was a delicate type, a fragrant phantom who every night floated into my room to check my breath. Not a woman who smoked and religiously watched Friday Night Fights.

Pearly clouds filled the living room, surrounded her. She dragged her Camel cigarette, tapped ashes into a drinking glass. On the TV, a rowdy crowd cheered. Three bells concluded the end of a round.

∴

One man strikes a lucky blow, the other falls down. Who doesn't love a man who gives himself up? More than amateur boxing, she favored visits with priests. One brought kielbasa and vodka. His forgiving eyes said sin was like rain, both absolved in nature.

In the next room, my grandmother brought her own nature. She folded her apron, a rosary coiled into a tiny snake in one of its pockets, crossed the straps, patted her hair. She unfastened one glass button – a black ladybug nested high between the leaf spreads of her collar.

∴

Just before her death, Grandmother dropped like a felled tree onto the floor of our living room. I woke to my mother's screams, to a dream of our house burning. Attendants guided her covered body on a stretcher.

At the cemetery, my father said *be very quiet; having missed you so much, hearing your voices might just kill her again.*

∴

She'd insisted grandchildren's voices were of an angelic choir; the silent ones needed the most cradling. Was I one of the angelic, one of the more silent ones? Sad music crackled through the funeral home speakers like fire.

Never again did God bleed summer rain, offer me nights of sunset-stain. Song swapped for a straight-to-the-back-of-the-throat shot of vodka, a mute peal of lavender pebble-shaped rosary beads. Asked *who, in the end, wins?* No one answered. A bell didn't ding. Tobacco dried up, left the ring.

They are all dead. I count slowly to six. I keep count in names, not numbers as I notice my fingers keeping a beat. Had I been able to see the coffins interred, neatly stacked, I could have counted by numbers instead. My maternal family – and here I can't come up with the right word – "live" in this gravesite underneath grass and dirt.

A fleeting thought that all I need is an incantation. Mix legitimate longing, aligned with two planets, on the fifth day of a leap year during a sleepy crescent moon to bring your family back to life. With the right spell, my family in a kit could materialize. It would have to be more elaborate than "just add water" or "assembly required." But in this fantasy, I embrace my Brujeria.

I replay faint scripts of cemetery visit rituals, and my adult feet weigh heavy and guilty. I am standing on top of my family. I don't resist the memories, the brain racket is familiar. My eyes are open but I can see the past: places, furniture, meals, and even hear a song from my childhood. The right side of my head pulses, a migraine approaches, maybe.

I sit down on the red granite bench my sister had installed a year ago. It looks nice but it's cold. Then a faint mist of water carried by the wind wakes me up enough to breathe deeply. I hear the sprinklers start their rhythmic cadence and watch long arches of water trying to resuscitate the fading Bermuda grass.

The birds have done quite a number on the sacred heart of Jesus no longer protected by the blue and white gingham Butter Crust bread bag Buelita tied violently with rubber bands around his neck. An unelegant solution, but it kept Jesus' cabezita protected from the urracas.

Cleaning is what comes next, but I don't visit like the eldest sibling does, with a bucket, a brush, and pruning shears to tame the anemic rose bushes flanking the grave that regardless of care, remain reddish, not red, thorny, and unapproachable. My ready-to-buy bouquet might have replaced wilted flowers, but the ones she brought still serve faithfully and perk out somewhat fresh. I stick my carnations into the mix of real and plastic flowers, inside the Folgers coffee can, wrapped in embossed gold foil. The makeshift vase is a chimera born of financial necessity, and seeing beauty and potential in the plainest of objects. Plus, thieves never bothered with a wrapped can.

Fixing my flowers, I'm distracted by street noise that wasn't here when I was a child. Traffic and sirens remind me that things change.

As a little girl, I came here with my grandparents on Sundays and holidays. It was quiet then at San Fernando Cemetery and much greener, like a park. I'd built up a thirst running and zigzagging through the small flat stone plates with people's names on them and drank from the sprinklers. Birds during the day and fireflies at dusk fluttered around and every once in a while, we saw butterflies. When the humid summers scorched us, we swatted mosquitoes, and at night counted our raised bumps to see who had the most bites.

The sky is clear. Anxious, my middle-aged brain reminds me I need to make a call or cross something off my neat list. I wrap my shawl tighter to keep the brief Texas winter air off my shoulders and look at the gravestone one more time. Hiking up my skirt, I try to kneel as close as I can, as if the sacred heart of Jesus marble can hear me. I want to speak something to make me believe in god again. I want to talk to them, all of them, but I can't. I want my mom. Mami. Half of my story laid to rest with them inside the ground.

On the channels of their carved names, I trace the letters with my index finger thinking that it might feel like writing in the sand. But the grooves are coarse and narrow, and my finger too big. The edges almost cut me and I let go. I am no longer kneeling, but sitting holding Jesus, one arm around his dirty neck, a drunken loose girl trying to tell an incomprehensible story after a party. I am half kneeling and half sitting hugging Jesus and tracing six names.

Oralia Torres Rocamontes... Juan Vaquera Rocamontes... Homero Juan Rocamontes... Gema Oralia Rocamontes... Maria De La Luz Rocamontes... Sergio Rolando Rocamontes.

I strip my name free of the American husbands and whisper...

Daphne Gema Santana Rocamontes.

I tell Henrietta about my father's mistress · Tina Barry

who called at 2 a.m., my mother snoring beside him. The phone rang in their room
and on the bedside table between my sister and me, a single siren's scream in the night.
I'd grab the receiver, cover it with my palm. Wrenched from sleep, we leaned in, heads
touching, bodies lit. No words, just their breathing; a language we didn't understand.
Once, her snort of laughter. Then months of nothing, until her last call at daybreak.
Whether she tried to lure him to love again, or offered a final serenade, I don't know.
But after his muffled '*ello*, we heard the clapper of the small bell she shook tinkling.

— we're all on a spectrum of woundedness
Dr. Gabor Maté

Before one light-bathed bench, a sun-crisped man, ageless,
Pads the iron slats with movers' blankets. Hoists his

Heft from a wheelchair, lays his body down. A burly woman
Perches on the bench beside his, fronted by a double-wide

Shopping cart, its contents covered with a fur coat.
White feathers float all around her, around the cart.

My mistaken eyes. Not angel feathers. Not
Eiderdown. Sudsy shampoo. She drips

Water from a plastic bottle —
Nowhere else to wash her hair.

Her neighbor taunts. The woman rises. Cart still
Conceals her front, boxwood blocks her back.

She continues her ablutions in the man's side
View. He hollers, *Pull up your pants you stupid-ass bitch,*

Hurling a plastic bottle her way. Misses.
She takes her mighty time. Scrubs, rinses, dries.

Clean & composed she strides forward, pushing
Her dignity. Down from his bench-bed he

Crawls hot macadam to retrieve his bottle,
His weapon. Her shower-bottle crammed back

Into her rolling home.   The spectrum of
Woundedness: along which we each carry

A bottle, a box, a blade or a bauble.

James Duncan · **Bailey's Hardware**

born ancient into this world
a two-story hardware store tilted
and faded with chipped paint like so
many autumn leaves falling red
yellow and brown from signs for
motor oil, chainsaws, Stanley, DeWalt,
Toro, barrels full of rakes out front,
Saturday afternoon collapsing into
sunset glinting off the 20 MPH sign, half
hidden to trap out-of-towners, tickets by
the dozen, and even locals couldn't stand
the townie Nassau cops who'd park
out of sight between Bailey's Hardware
and the Sunoco station, a single island
with one pump for diesel, one for unleaded,
$1.59 a gallon sign overhead, askew and
rusted, born ancient into this world
and not getting any younger as Saturday
night succumbs to Sunday, one red light
flashing silent in the center of town,
an intersection to nowhere, no way out,
just red lights reflected all night in the
windows of Bailey's Hardware store, nuts &
bolts, work gloves half-off, waiting just for you
to come and bring them anywhere else
and give them purpose, give them life

Snow at Louveciennes by Alfred Sisley, 1878 · Donna Pucciani

Museee d'Orsay, Paris

Awash in white, winter speaks
the silent language of deep snow,
entombing everything in sight –

the carpeted country path, the roofs
of modest dwellings on either side,
the boughs of trees leaning into each other,
laden with the disembodied ghosts
of last night's blizzard.

Between stone walls shouldering the weight
of pale greenish drifts, walks a thin, solitary figure,
black on white, aiming for what appears to be
a dead end, her dark cloak an ebony sigh.

The church tower floats overhead
in the vaguely gray sky, its muted bells
looming like the phantom invitations
of angels.

I'm sorry,   hatchling,   cheeping up at me   from the   rain-damped path.

    I'm not the kind of woman
    to nurse a fallen chick
    with an eyedropper.

To my credit, I do trouble myself   to catch you,   chasing your frantic,   unfledged
hop until you tire;   to gather you gently,   as if you still wore an eggshell's fragile   swaddle;
to re-nest you   in laurel bush branches, where you'll be safe, at least, from the next   fox,
if not from the fox after that.   Because I'm selfish,   I leave you this way,
and make it all about me,   this spuriously-tender death postponement,
revisiting past selves –   millions of microscopic, momentary "me"s   shed   like skin cells.

    I've been the kind of woman
    to break a jar in the store
    and walk away.
    The kind
    to poach another's entrée
    from the work fridge.

Such transient, uncomely selves linger   with the life-outlasting span   of bad photos.

    I've also been the kind
    to step in and translate for an elderly couple
    at an impasse with the pharmacist;

To drive twenty miles
to repatriate a driver license
plucked from a gas station bathroom floor.

These finer selves left   brighter,   nobler   traces,
quite unkin to the one that abandons you,   hatchling,   to your fate.
Could be that suckling three infants   drained my compassion   for helpless things.
Or that I'm not my best today.   Just tired.   Or worse, inspired?

I'm afraid that's it,   little bird.

I'm the kind of woman who,
on finding a tumbled chick,
moans and coos as if she cares

when really, in her ruthless,   artful   brain,
        she's thinking already of how she will bake you –
                feathers, feet, and all your   doomed sweet –
                                into the pie   of a poem.

Crystal Karlberg · **Yellow Is The Light**

after *Red Hill and White Shell, 1938* by Georgia O'Keeffe

Moon snail shell. I have held
something similar and marveled
at the continuous opening to life.
Curve of shoulder, of elbow, fingers
curled, head tucked creating
an infinite spiral. In the soft tissue
of the hill: protection.

The red paint is bright in places
not the dark blood that drenches,
but the bright, first kind, the signal
of release. There is even a small
patch of green at the horizon
for the door that changed everything.
Yellow is the light spilled
on the sidewalk from a single window.

My father's face was pink
and then crimson when he was screaming.
What if everyone's pain
is a different color?
*Your mother always wanted
a son,* my father loved

to tell me, not knowing
the whole story,
not even knowing
the half of it.

Ki Russell · **Mosaic**

"Only fragments are accurate"
– Lyn Hejinian

Drag your fingers
                        through my shards.

Let my fragments
                        pool around
        you.   Some of the edges

        are sharp and you'll
                learn to brush your fingers
across them.

Others have blunted
                        from decades abrading them.

You can hook
                        your fingers
between   them   and   draw
me   apart   again.

Misreading leads me to sundry wonders · Annie Stenzel

Like the time I read the Audre Lorde line

love is a word another kind of open

just a little wrong
and thought it said

love is a new kind of apron

which in one sense I guess it can be:
a robust amour-propre can help
keep the world's worst soil

off my fancy outfit. After all
these years solo, I am not the object
of anyone else's ardor – I must lap

myself with suitable expressions
of affection to avoid
the cold stain of indifference.

Which is not always
an easy job. Once bloom and beauty
wane, the knee-jerk of *ooh-love*

and *ah-love* from other quarters
dwindles. But the original pump
for this essence may simply

want priming. Get to work
beneath the apron. A half-teaspoon
of self-love siphoned into your pocket

may turn out to be
plenty.

we'd kissed for fleshly return · Jill Pearlman

Laid up, ill

oh prickly one, with your autumn fruit

and blistered lips burned in the desert sun,

who scaled hills like a goat before taking off your boots

in a room where language runs to millimeters, grams, syringes,

squaring off against fluorescent light so bright it frightens.

We'd kissed for fleshly return, not faux transcendence.

The nurse questioned me about your skin: where is it war-torn, ragged –

I scan lips, cheeks fragrant with crushed seeds and leaves,

fingertips, penis, tubes making loops,

come circle full to your feet, unshod, tender, cracked.

Is there anything more, nurse.

I ask your openhearted soles and gorgeous metatarsals to hold earth close.

Mark Belair · **the cord**

a long / dangling / loop of cord / frayed and stretched to near-breaking / has served
generations of sextons and priests / wishing to open the high / stained glass windows /
whose warrior angels / bearing swords and breastplates / overlook

this gothic church filled with statues of / saints / loyal apostles / roman soldiers / kings
and emperors / early church fathers / the virgin mary at the annunciation / christ
cradling his sacred heart / christ nailed to a splintered cross / and of the damned amid
flames / in poses of grief and shame / near a saint who lies in peace / beside a jeweled
box of his relics

yet it's the worn / but still working cord / that calls me to worship

Author Biographies

R. A. Allen's poetry has appeared in the *New York Quarterly, B O D Y, The Penn Review, RHINO, The Los Angeles Review*, and elsewhere. His work has been nominated for a Best of the Net and two Pushcarts. He lives in Memphis.

◎

Toni Artuso (she/her/hers) is an emerging/aging trans female writer from Salem, Massachusetts. Her verse has appeared in *Honeyguide Literary Magazine*, which nominated one of her pieces for a Pushcart Prize. Her poems have also appeared in *The Christian Science Monitor, Salamander, The Cackling Kettle, The Lyric*, and *Star*Line*.

◎

Subhaga Crystal Bacon (she/her) is a Queer poet living in rural Washington on unceded Methow land. She is the author of four collections of poetry including *Surrender of Water in Hidden Places* from Red Flag Poetry, and *Transitory*, forthcoming in the fall from BOA Editions.

Cynthia Bargar is Associate Poetry editor at *Pangyrus*. Her poems have appeared in many journals including *Nixes Mate, SWWIM Every Day, Driftwood Press, Rogue Agent, Book of Matches, LUMINA* and in the book, *Our Provincetown: Intimate Portraits by Barbara E. Cohen* (Provincetown Arts Press, 2021). Her poetry collection, *Sleeping in the Dead Girl's Room*, came out from Lily Poetry Review Books in 2022. Cynthia lives with her partner, cartoonist Nick Thorkelson, in Provincetown, Massachusetts.

◉

Tina Barry is the author of *Beautiful Raft* and *Mall Flower*. Her writing appeared in *Nixes Mate, Rattle, Verse Daily, The Best Small Fictions 2020* (spotlighted story) and 2016, *Trampset, A-Minor, Unbroken, Gone Lawn, The Maryland Literary Journal, South Florida Poetry Journal* and *Flash-Frontier*. Tina teaches at The Poetry Barn and Writers.com.

◉

Mark Belair has published in numerous journals, including *Alabama Literary Review, Harvard Review,* and *Michigan Quarterly Review*. He is the author of seven collections of poems. His most recent books are two works of fiction: *Stonehaven* (Turning Point, 2020) and its sequel, *Edgewood* (Turning Point, 2022). Find more at www.markbelair.com

◉

Shari Caplan (she/her) is the artist behind *Exhibitionist* (forthcoming, Lily Poetry Review Books, Paul Nemser Prize Winner), *The Red Shoes; a Phantasmagoric Ballet on Paper*, (Lambhouse Books), and *Advice from a Siren* (Dancing Girl Press). Her poems have swum into *Gulf Coast, Painted Bride Quarterly, Sinister Wisdom,* and others. Find out more at ShariCaplan.com.

Rebecca Connors is the author of the chapbook, *Split Map* (Minerva Rising Press, 2019). Her poems can be found in *DIALOGIST, Glass Poetry Journal*, and *Tinderbox Poetry Journal*, among others. She is the co-founder of *The Notebooks Collective* and lives in Boston with her family and two cats.

◉

James H Duncan is the editor of *Hobo Camp Review* and the author of *We Are All Terminal But This Exit Is Mine, Vacancy*, and *Berlin*, among other collections. He currently resides in upstate New York and reviews indie bookshops at The Bookshop Hunter blog. For more, visit jameshduncan.com.

◉

Laura Gamache, a Seattle poet and teaching artist, has published in journals and anthologies, including *Passager Journal 2022, Rattle, Altered Syntax, So, Dear Writer*, and *WA129*, and in her chapbooks, *Never Enough* and *Nothing to Hold Onto*. She has worked in Puget Sound area classrooms as a WITS writer since 1997.

◉

Alexis Ivy is a 2018 recipient of the Massachusetts Cultural Council Fellowship in Poetry. She is the author of *Romance with Small-Time Crooks* (BlazeVOX [books], 2013), and *Taking the Homeless Census* (Saturnalia Books, 2020) which won the 2018 Saturnalia Editors Prize. Her poems have recently appeared in *Saranac Review, Poet Lore* and *Sugar House Review*. She lives in her hometown Boston, working as an advocate for the homeless and teaching in the PoemWorks community.

Natalie Jill's most recent work has appeared or is upcoming in *Free State Review, Oakland Review, Atlanta Review*, and *Sugar House Review*. She is a member of the PoemWorks community in the Boston area.

◉

Crystal Karlberg is a Library Assistant at her local public library in Massachusetts. Her poems have been published or are forthcoming in: *Threepenny Review; Beloit Poetry Journal; Penn Review; Lily Poetry Review; oddball magazine.*

◉

Francesca Leader has poetry published or forthcoming in *Door is a Jar, the Sho Poetry Journal, Frost Meadow Review, Harpy Hybrid Review, Pluvia Litmag, Roi Fainéant, the Stoneboat Literary Journal, Bullshit Lit, Cutbow Quarterly*, and elsewhere. Her translation of an ancient Japanese poem won the Society of Classical Poets' 2021 Poetry Translation Competition. Learn more about her work at inabucketthebook.wordpress.com.)

◉

Deborah Leipziger is an author, poet, and advisor on sustainability. Born in Brazil, Deborah's poems have been published in eight countries. Deborah's new book, *Story & Bone*, was published by Lily Poetry Review Books. She is the author of several books on human rights and sustainability

◉

Sara Letourneau is a poet, book editor, writing coach, and the cofounder of the Pour Me a Poem open mic in Mansfield, Massachusetts. Her poetry appears in *Amethyst Review, Soul-Lit, Full Mood Mag, Arlington*

Literary Journal, *Muddy River Poetry Review*, and Constellations, among others. Visit Sara online at heartofthestoryeditorial.com.

◉

Kerry Loughman is a retired educator and photographer living in the Boston area. She writes about memory, art, family, and nature in the city, (looking for small transient moments of beauty, or discord.)Her work has appeared in Mass Poetry's *The Hard Work of Hope*, *Nixes Mate*, *What Rough Beast*, and *The Main Street Rag*.

◉

Jennifer Martelli is the author of *The Queen of Queens* and *My Tarantella* both chosen as "Must Reads" by the Massachusetts Center for the Book. Her work has appeared in *Poetry*, *The Academy of American Poets Poem-a-Day*, and elsewhere. Jennifer Martelli has twice received grants from the Massachusetts Cultural Council and is co-poetry editor for *Mom Egg Review*.

◉

David P. Miller's collection, *Bend in the Stair*, was published by Lily Poetry Review Books in 2021. *Sprawled Asleep* was published by Nixes Mate Books in 2019. His poems have appeared in *Meat for Tea*, *Solstice*, *Lily Poetry Review*, *Kestrel*, *subTerrain*, *Constellations*, *Jerry Jazz Musician*, *Last Stanza*, and *LEON Literary Review*, among others.

◉

Gloria Monaghan is a Professor at Wentworth University. She has published six books of poetry. Her most recent collection, *Cormorant on the Strand* was published by Lily Poetry Review (2023). Her poems have appeared in *Alexandria Quarterly, NPR, Poem-a-Day, Lily Poetry Review, Mom Egg Review*, among others. She has been nominated for the Pushcart Prize, the Massachusetts Book Award, and the Griffin Prize.

Phil Montenegro's poetry has appeared in Yale School of Divinity's *LETTERS Journal, Nixes Mate Review, Caliban, The Tower Journal, Otoliths, The Pierian, PoemTown 22/23, Poem City 23, Ayris Magazine*, and *Tidepools Magazine* where his poem "Eleven A.M." won first prize for their 50th edition.

◉

Ammanda Selethia Moore is a non-binary poet and writer who also teaches English at Norco College. Their poetry has been published in *DASH Literary Journal, Literary Yard*, and *The Journal of Radical Wonder*. They live with their partner in sunny southern California.

◉

Miriam O'Neal's poetry has appeared in *Blackbird Journal, North Dakota Quarterly, The Waxed Lemon, Galway Review*, and elsewhere. Her third collection of poems is *The Half-Said Things* (Nixes Mate 2022). She hosts Poetry the Art of Word, a monthly reading series in Plymouth, MA, where she lives and writes and listens to birds singing.

◉

Dzvinia Orlowsky has published six poetry collections including *Bad Harvest*, a 2019 Massachusetts Book Award "Must Read" in Poetry. Her co-translations with Ali Kinsella of Natalka Bilotserkivets's poems, *Eccentric Days of Hope and Sorrow*, (Lost Horse Press, 2021), was a finalist for the 2022 Griffin Poetry Prize and winner of the AAUS Translation Prize.

Jill Pearlman is a Rhode Island-based poet exploring ecstasy in the decentered self and world. Her poems have appeared in *Salamander, Barrow Street, The Common, Ocean State Review, Crosswinds, Soul-Lit, Indicia.* She has produced several multimedia poetry series: "Trees Road Vertigo," and "Mirrors: A Conversation with Avivah Zornberg."

◉

Donna Pucciani, a Chicago-based writer, has published poetry worldwide in *Shi Chao Poetry, Li Poetry, Poetry Salzburg, Agenda, Gradiva, Meniscus, Poetry on the Lake,* and other journals. Her seventh and latest collection of poems is *EDGES.*

◉

Brad Rose is the author of five collections of poetry and flash fiction: *Lucky Animals, No. Wait. I Can Explain., Pink X-Ray, de/tonations, Momentary Turbulence,* and *WordInEdgeWise.* He has published in, *The Los Angeles Times, The American Journal of Poetry, New York Quarterly, Puerto del Sol, Baltimore Review, , Lunch Ticket, Sequestrum, Unbroken, Cultural Daily,* and other publications. His website is bradrosepoetry.com

◉

Ki Russell teaches writing, literature, and creative writing at Blue Mountain Community College in Pendleton, Oregon. She is the author of *Antler Woman Responds* (Paladin), *The Wolf at the Door* (Ars Omnia), and *How to Become Baba Yaga* (Medulla). She also serves as poetry peer reviewer for *Whale Road Review.* Her poems have been published in many online and print journals.

◉

Daphne Santana Strassmann writes about the intangible spaces between her Latino heritage and American life. She is a professor of creative writing and founder of "Rekindle Your Craft," a generative writing workshop. She is completing a collection of essays, written in Spanglish, her most faithful narrative voice, titled *Domexican Gringa*.

◉

Sarah Dickenson Snyder's collections include *The Human Contract* (2017), *Notes from a Nomad* (nominated for the Massachusetts Book Awards 2018), and *With a Polaroid Camera* (2019), and *Now These Three Remain* forthcoming (2023). She's had Best of Net and Pushcart Prize nominations. Recent work is in *Rattle, Lily Poetry Review*, and *RHINO*. sarah-dickensonsnyder.com

◉

Annie Stenzel's (she/her) poems appear in *Atlanta Review, Chestnut Review, FERAL, K'in, Nixes Mate, On The Seawall, Lily Poetry Review, rust + moth, SWWIM, The Lake, Thimble*, and *Third Wednesday*, among other journals. She lives on unceded Ohlone land within walking distance of the San Francisco Bay.

◉

Meghan Sterling's work is forthcoming in *The Los Angeles Review, Rhino Poetry, Meridian, Hunger Mountain* and many others. *Self-Portrait with Ghosts of the Diaspora* (Harbor Editions), *Comfort the Mourners* (Everybody Press) and *View from a Borrowed Field* (Lily Poetry Review's Paul Nemser Book Prize) are out in 2023.

◉

Tim Suermondt's sixth full-length book of poems *A Doughnut And The Great Beauty Of The World* came out early in 2023 from MadHat Press. He has published in *Poetry, Ploughshares, Prairie Schooner, The Georgia*

Review, Bellevue Literary Review, Stand Magazine, Nixes Mate, Smartish Pace, The Fortnightly Review, Poet Lore and *Plume*, among many others. He lives in Cambridge (MA) with his wife, the poet Pui Ying Wong.

◉

Susan Isla Tepper is the author of 11 published books of fiction and poetry, and two stage plays. Her newest novel titled *Hair Of A Fallen Angel* will be published in early 2024. susantepper.com

◉

Cindy Veach's most recent book *Her Kind* (CavanKerry Press) was named a finalist for the 2022 Eric Hoffer Montaigne Medal. She is also the author of *Gloved Against Blood* (CavanKerry Press) a finalist for the Paterson Poetry Prize and a Massachusetts Center for the Book 'Must Read,' and the chapbook, *Innocents* (Nixes Mate). Her poems have appeared in the *Academy of American Poets Poem-a-Day, AGNI, Michigan Quarterly Review, Poet Lore, The Journal,* and *Salamander* among others. She is the recipient of the Philip Booth Poetry Prize and the Samuel Allen Washington Prize. Cindy is co-poetry editor of *MER*. cindyveach.com

◉

Allya Yourish is from Portland, Oregon and currently living in Ames, Iowa. She has two cats that keep her heart filled with joy and a big bookcase that keeps her brain buzzing with poems. She was a nanny in Paris, France, a Fulbright grantee in Kuala Krau, Malaysia, a news assistant for the New York Times, and now she is getting her MFA in Creative Writing and the Environment from Iowa State University.

Colophon

The text is set in Maiola, a contemporary typeface inspired by early Czech type design. The titles are set in Tablet Gothic, a grotesque sans-serif grounded in 19th century British typography. Both fonts were designed by Veronika Burian, a type designer and co-founder of the independent type foundry TypeTogether. She is also involved with Alphabettes.org, a showcase for work and research on lettering, typography, and type design by women.